AutoCA

Starter Pack

For Secondary Students

ROMARIO CHAMBERS

Preface

The purpose of this book is to provide secondary school students with a practical approach to the theory and application of AutoCAD.

This book should prove useful to those learning the program for the first time as it provides a good foundation for students taking the Engineering and Architectural course.

In this book, a holistic approach was taken to cover the basic steps for the use of commands, control, and parameters of AutoCAD.

This book can be used as a class guide or as a self-study workbook.

A good understanding of the information in this book will provide a solid foundation for using the AutoCAD program at the highest level.

Table of Content

What is AutoCAD?

The acronym AutoCAD stands for Computer-Aided Design (CAD).

AutoCAD is a computer program designed to perform all the tasks that can be done by conventional (manual) drawing.

Starting AutoCAD

You can start AutoCAD by either double clicking on the program icon on the desktop or by clicking on the program name in the Start menu. The program will start. The monitor will display a screen similar to the one shown below.

Once you start a new drawing or continue to work with an existing drawing, your screen will access the drawing editor as displayed.

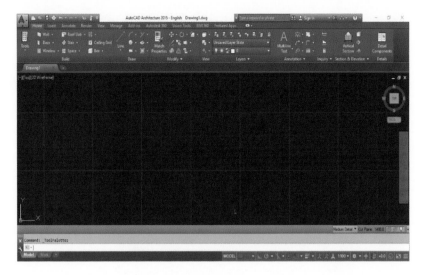

If you are already in the drawing editor and wish to continue working on a drawing that is already existing, click on the "A" icon in the extreme upper left corner of the window and then select Open->Drawing.

A "Select File" dialog box will open which will allow you to select the drawing file you want to open.

To start a new drawing when the drawing editor is already open, use the following steps.

1. Click on the "A" icon

2. Select the tab that says New. Upon selecting this tab, the program will take you directly to a new drawing sheet.

Elements of the User Interface

- Title bar
- Pull-down menu bar
- Standard toolbar
- Layer toolbar
- Properties toolbar
- Styles toolbar
- Draw toolbar
- Modify toolbar
- Command line window
- Status bar

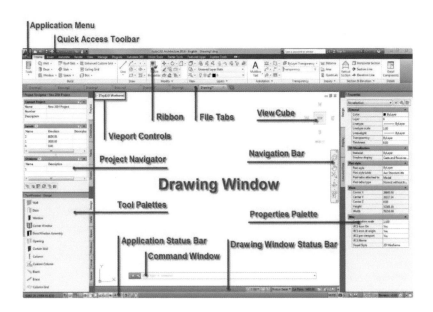

Setting up Drawing Environment

Before beginning a drawing, you are required to set up your work area. Carry out these basic steps to set up the area;

1. Determine and set _units_ to be used.
2. Determine and set drawing _limits_; then _zoom all._
3. Set appropriate _snap_ type and increment.
4. Set appropriate _grid_ value to be used.

Limits

Limits specify the outer boundaries or edges of your drawing area in X, Y units. The lower-left corner limit is universal and is always set at default 0,0. The upper-right corner defines the size of the drawing area.

Steps to set drawing limits:

1. Type *limits*.
2. Specify lower-left corner 0,0, press enter.
3. Specify upper-right corner, press enter.
4. Type zoom (z) enter, all (a) enter. *This allows the user to move around the work space freely.*
5. Click OK.

Saving Dwg Files

Saving AutoCAD files is quite simple. Use the following steps to save your file correctly.

1. Click Application Menu ➤ Save As ➤ Other Formats ➤ Find

2. In the Save Drawing As dialog box of the File Name box, enter a new drawing name.

3. Under Files of type, select the AutoCAD file format you want.

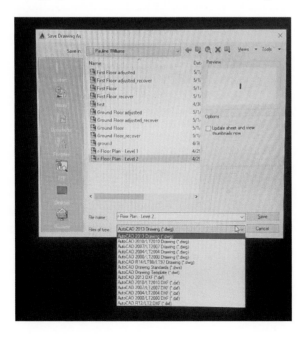

Note: AutoCAD files saved with a later version can pose a challenge for users with an earlier version to open. It is recommended that if a later version is being used, the file should be saved in a format compatible with earlier versions. This is done in the drop down menu. Select an earlier year and hit "Save".

Saving DWG files to PDF

Sometimes drawing needs to be saved in a format that is not a ".dwg" extension. There are other file formats in which drawings can be saved. One of the most commonly used format is PDF. You save drawings in pdf when you are preparing to plot a drawing or present to a client.

Here are some simple steps to plot drawing as PDF:

1. Open print menu.
2. Select printer/plotter.
3. Select your paper size.
4. Adjust plot scale and center your drawing.
5. Select drawing orientation.
6. Select whether to plot by display, limits or window under plot area.
7. Press Ok.

Note: If using paper space, plotting a PDF file as a soft copy once page size, orientation, and scale has been set would only be required to select print options and drawing orientation.

Units

What are units?

A unit is any standard used for comparison in measurements. Units allow you to specify the type and precision of linear and angular measurements and also direction and orientation of angles in drawing.

Using this command, you can set the drawing units and other settings like the precision of linear and angular dimensions and default rotation angle.

To access this menu, type units and hit enter.

Status Bar

The AutoCAD status bar displays cursor location, drawing tools and tools affecting your drawing's environment. The status bar also gives quick access to some of the tools more commonly used.

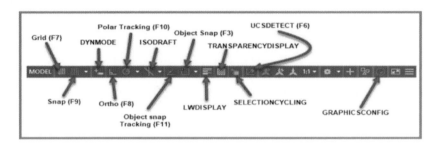

F7

This status bar tool will toggle the visibility of the background grid which is often visible in your drawing area.

F9

Toggle Snap mode: when snap mode is active, AutoCAD cursor will jump to specific points in the drawing area which is defined in snap mode.

F8

Toggles Ortho mode on and off. When ortho mode is on, you can make lines either horizontally or vertically.

Line weight display

This system variable toggles visibility of line weight in a drawing. The default value of this system variable is OFF. You can change its value to ON to keep line weight visible in the drawing area.

F3

This function key activates or deactivates object snap option. When object snap is active, you will be able to snap your cursor to some exact points in the geometry like end, center, quadrant, tangent, etc. This option allows you to make precise AutoCAD drawings.

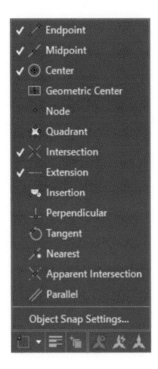

Endpoint

The ending point of a line.

Midpoint

This is the center or middle of a line.

Center

This is the center of a circle or an arc.

Intersection

This is the point where two lines cross each other.

Parallel

Two lines running alongside each other in one direction.

Perpendicular

Two lines running in opposite directions forming a right angle where they meet.

Layers

Auto CAD gives you the option to separate classes of objects into layers.

The layer panel has a dropdown list for making layer control quickly and easily. The list displays the current layers name, visibility setting, and properties. Selecting any layer's name makes it current.

To set the layers:

1. Pick the layer property manager icon

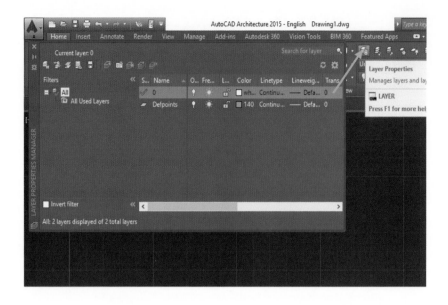

2. Pick the new layer button

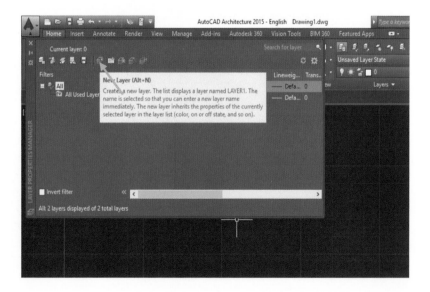

3. Type the name of the layer (e.g. Outline)

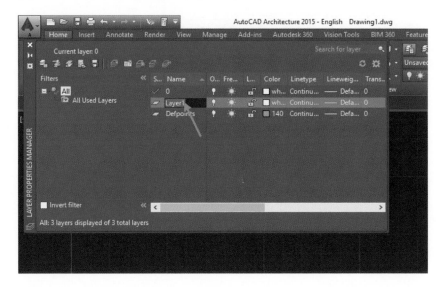

4. Select linetype, lineweight, and color.

Color, linetype, and lineweight

Layers have properties of color, linetype, and lineweight. It is possible to assign a specific color, linetype, and lineweight to an object which will override the color, linetype, and lineweight layers.

Color

When creating a layer, you are required to select a specific color for your layer. By clicking on the color, you can open a *color dialog window*. Upon opening the color dialog window, you can select from a variety of colors by simply clicking on a color.

21

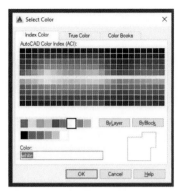

Linetype

To specify the linetype after creating a layer, you can click on the line that's in the linetype column. A dialog box will open displaying the different types of lines needed based on the required drawing. If the linetype needed isn't displayed, you can load more lines by clicking load at the bottom of the window.

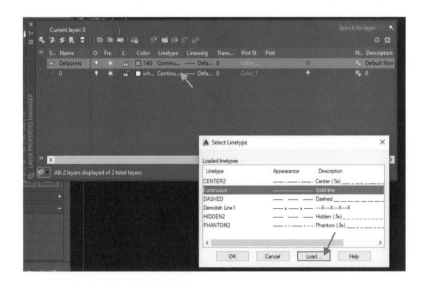

Lineweight

The lineweight can be set by selecting the lineweight option in the lineweight column in the layer property list. By selecting that option, the lineweight dialog box will open. This allows you to select from a wide range of sizes.

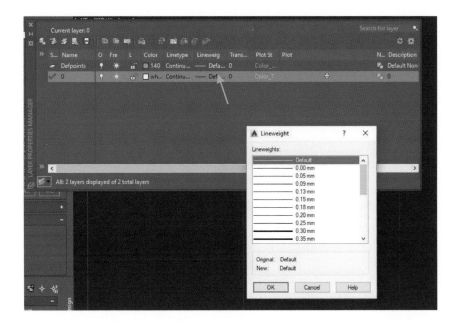

Keyboard Shortcuts

Ctrl + N

You can use this shortcut to open a new drawing tab in AutoCAD.

Ctrl + S

You can use this keyboard shortcut to save a drawing file.

Ctrl + Shift + S

You can use this keyboard shortcut to save the drawing as a new file. It is also used as the "Save As" command.

Ctrl + 0

Clears screen to show only the drawing area; hides palettes and tabs. Press it twice to reset the default AutoCAD interface.

Ctrl + 2

Can be used to open the design center palette which contains many AutoCAD blocks that can be used in your drawing.

Ctrl + 9

You can use this keyboard shortcut to toggle the visibility of the command line. If for some reason your command line is hidden from the drawing area, then use this keyboard shortcut to bring it back.

This reflects the commands entered in the program while drawing.

Ctrl + C

You can use this to copy objects. First, select objects from the drawing area, then press Ctrl + C to copy objects to the clipboard.

Ctrl + V

This is used to paste copied objects while keeping their original properties.

Ctrl + Shift + V

This shortcut is used to paste copied objects as block.

Ctrl + Z

Used to undo the last action in your drawing. You can press this shortcut key multiple times to undo many actions.

Ctrl + Y

This keyboard shortcut can be used to redo the last undo action which you have performed.

Dimension

Dimensions are considered an annotative object. This means dimensions are scale-dependent when plotted from paper space. Paper space is where you place a drawing to get it accurately positioned on a sheet for plotting.

Dimension Style

Dimension styles (dimstyle) are used to manage and automate every aspect of your dimensions. It allows you to maintain consistency in your drawing annotations and to organize your dimensions.

Every characteristic of your dimensions is controlled by the dimension style. This includes symbols, arrows, text height, and units. Dimension style objects are any objects used to add information to a drawing.

Dimension style provides information about features such as the length of a wall the diameter of a circle and even a detail callout. Annotations are scaled differently from the drawing; they are dependent on how they should appear when plotted.

AutoCAD organizes dimension style settings into convenient tabs as shown below.

To locate dimension style:

1. Type dimstyle, hit enter, and then select modify.

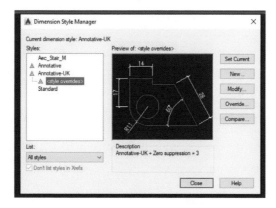

2. Modify settings for different tabs as required.

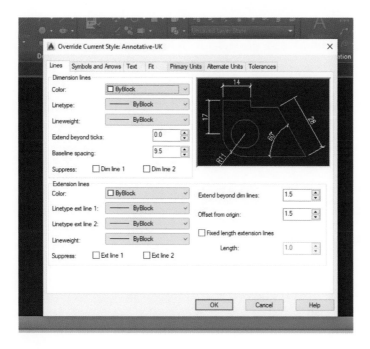

3. Select OK.

Types of Dimension

Linear Dimension Command

Linear dimension commands are used to add dimension along straight lines. When using linear dimension, specify the two points where you want the dimension to be drawn and pick a point to fix the position of the dimension.

The Continue Dimension Command

The Continue command can be used to add a string of dimensions. By using the Continue command, you can quickly generate a string of dimension that is perfectly aligned. You can only continue a dimension in one direction.

Note: AutoCAD automatically selects the origin of the previous dimension to be the first new dimension.

Aligned Dimension Command

Aligned dimensions are used to add dimension along inclined lines which cannot be dimensioned by linear dimension. This is because linear dimension is used strictly for linear and vertical dimensioning.

Hatch

A hatch is a tool which fills an enclosed area or selected objects with a pattern, solid or gradient fill. Hatching is used to portray that an area of a drawing has a particular attribute.

Hatches can be used to signify different things. Hatches can:

- Show surface finish or pattern.
- Show that a section is cut through a certain part of a building or material.
- Differentiate between an existing or proposed part of a building.

Steps to carry out hatching:

1. Select Hatch. The *Hatch Type list* will appear, select the type of hatch you want to use.

2. On the Pattern panel, click a hatch pattern or fill.

3. On the Boundaries panel, specify how the pattern boundary is selected:

4. Pick Points: this inserts the hatch or fill within a closed area that is bounded by one or more objects. With this method, you click within the boundaries to specify the area.

5. Select Boundary Objects: This inserts the hatch or fill within a closed object, such as a circle, closed polyline, or a set of objects with endpoints that touch and enclose an area.

6. The selection method is retained until you change it.

7. Click an area or object to be hatched.

8. On the ribbon, make any adjustments as needed:

Tool Palettes

Tools palettes can be used to create libraries of frequently used blocks, tools, and commands for easy access. The default tool palette has frequently used blocks readily available. You can also create your own tool palette and organize your blocks into different groups.

To launch tool palettes, press CTRL + 3 or in the command line you can type TP.

To create a tool palette, right-click on any palette and select *New Palette*. Assign a name and hit enter. When adding tools to a tool palette, you can:

- Drag tools such as dimensions, fills, blocks and tables from your drawing.
- Drag drawings, blocks, or hatches from *design center*.
- Paste tools from one palette to another.

Blocks

Blocks are a collection of geometry that form a single shape. They can be used in a drawing repetitively. The blocks used in a drawing are called block references. Blocks can be a plain and simple collection of static geometry.

To insert a block, you:

1. Type insert into the command line and hit enter.

2. The dialog box will appear. Enter the name of the block you are searching for.

3. Press enter.

WBlocks

WBlocks allows you to save selected objects or convert a block to a specified drawing file.

Entering *wblock* at the Command prompt displays a standard file selection dialog box. In this box, specify a name for the new drawing file. The new drawing is saved in the file format that is specified in Save As on the Open and Save tab in the Options dialog box.

In the new drawing, the world coordinate system (WCS) is set parallel to the user coordinate system (UCS).

The following prompts are displayed.

Name of output file
Specifies the path and name of the output file.

Existing block
Saves the specified objects to an existing block file. You cannot enter the name of an external reference (xref) or one of its dependent blocks.

Define new drawing
Saves the objects to a new drawing file.

- = . Specifies that the existing block and the output file have the same name.
- *. Writes the entire drawing to the new output file, except for unreferenced symbols. Model space objects are written to model space, and paper space objects are written to paper space.

Design Center

Design center is used to organize access to drawings, hatches, blocks, and other drawing content.

Using design center, allows you to:

- Browse for drawing content such as drawings or symbol libraries.
- View definition tables for blocks and layers in a drawing file and then insert, attach, copy and paste the definitions into a current drawing.
- Update (redefine) a block definition.
- Open drawing files in a new window.
- Drag drawings, blocks, and hatches to a tool palette for convenient access.
- Copy and paste content, such as layer definitions, layouts, and text styles between open drawings.

Design Center Window

You can use the tree view on the left to browse sources of content and to display content in the content area on the right. From the content area, you can add items to a drawing or to a tool palette. A preview or description is displayed for selected drawings, blocks, and hatch patterns.

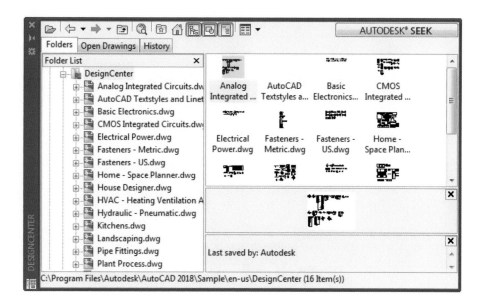

The Design Center toolbar controls navigation and display of information in the tree view and the content area. The same navigation and display options are available on the shortcut menu.

Basic Drawing Tools

Line

Creates straight line segments.

Polyline

A polyline is made of numerous lines, arcs, or both, segmented together into one selectable object. Polylines are versatile and the PEDIT (Polyline Edit) command can be used to access and edit many of the features associated with them.

Rectangle

This is a quick way of drawing a four-segment polyline with four right angles.

Arc

An arc is a circle segment defined by selecting three points. Alternatively, the user can define a center point, a radius, and a range of degrees to fill.

Circle

The only variables here are radius and center point; the shortcut to use this function is "C".

Spline

Spline is used to create a smooth curve that passes through or near specified points.

Ellipse

Ellipse is an oval that requires a radius to be defined for both their vertical and horizontal components.

Hatch

Hatches are area fills. Hatches can be applied to a particular object such as a looped polyline or any enclosed area.

Text

Inserts a text string into the drawing. AutoCAD uses two forms of text entries: single line and multiline. These are known respectively as DTEXT and MTEXT.

Basic Modifying Tools

Erase

Erases the selected object from the drawing. Can also be activated by pressing the delete key on the keyboard.

Copy

Copies a selected object from one point on the drawing to one or more locations.

Mirror

Creates a mirror image of the selected objects. The user defines two points, AutoCAD then generates a "line of reflection" and the reflected object is generated across this line with all components reversed.

Offset

Offset is used to duplicate an object at a specified distance from its original position.

Array

An array is a quick way of copying multiple objects once all the copies are arranged in a linear way.

Move

Moves an object to a specified distance or location.

Rotate

Rotates an object around a specific center point or based on a given or desired angle.

Scale

Enlarges or reduces selected objects while maintaining the proportions of the object after scaling.

Trim

This command is used for trimming a geometry.

AutoCAD Shortcut Keys

Basic Drawings Tools

Symbols	Commands	Shortcuts
Line	Line	L + enter
Polyline	Polyline	PL + enter
Rectangle	Rectangle	REC+ enter
Arc	Arc	A + enter
Circle	Circle	C + enter
Spline	Spline	SPL + enter
Ellipse	Ellipse	EL + enter
Hatch	Hatch	H + enter
Text	Text	T + enter

AutoCAD Shortcut Keys

Basic Modifying Tools

Symbols	Commands	Shortcuts
	Erase	Erase + enter
Copy	Copy	CO + enter
Mirror	Mirror	MI + enter
	Offset	O + enter
Array	Array	AR + enter
Move	Move	M + enter
Rotate	Rotate	RO + enter
Scale	Scale	SC + enter
Trim	Trim	TR + enter x 2

Canceling a Command

If you start a command and do not want to complete it, you can press the Esc key to cancel the command. For some commands, you may have to press the Esc key more than once. Keep pressing the Esc key until you see the Command prompt at the bottom of the screen.

Plotting from Model Space to Layout

In the bottom left hand corner of the drawing area, you will see a model tab and two layout tabs. Whenever you access AutoCAD to begin a drawing, the *Model tab* is active by default. Objects that represent the subject of a drawing are normally drawn in *Model tab*. Model tab is also known as model space.

A layout tab can be activated by selecting *Layout1* or *Layout2* of any other layout tab. A layout is a representation of the paper used to plot a drawing. It is sometimes referred to as paper space. The dashed line around the sheet tells the maximum printable area for the configure plotter. Multiple layouts can be done with each one representing a different sheet size or plotter.

Layout setup

In order to properly organize a layout or paper space, you are advised to properly set up your space to facilitate the different amenities needed. Carry out the following basic steps to set up your layout;

1. Select layout tab in the bottom left hand corner.
2. Right click on the layout tab and select *page setup manager.*
3. From the page setup dialog, click *modify.*
4. In the page setup dialog, select your *plotter, paper size,* and *plot style.*
5. Select Ok and close the page setup manager.

6. You can now create your title block or import a title block and add your information.

7. If you wish to remove the viewport available and reintroduce it later, you may do so. *(Optional)*

Note: *To plot a drawing in PDF, under the plotter drop down menu select the option DWG to PDF.*

A viewport is automatically created when you activate a layout. A viewport is a window that looks into the model space. Therefore, you first create the drawing in model space, then you activate a layout and create a viewport to look into model space. Only drawing objects such as border, title block, and some text are created in layout.

Steps to setup a viewport:

1. Use the *Rectangle tool* to create a rectangle in paper space.
2. Select the *layout tab* on the ribbon at the top of the screen.
3. Under the *layout tab* in the *layout viewports* section, click on the arrow below the heading labelled *Rectangle* and select *Object*.
4. Select the rectangle drawn in *step 1*. The viewport is now active.

Scaling a Drawing

The view of a drawing that appears in the viewport is scaled to achieve the desired print scale. You can control the scale of the drawing by setting the viewport scale.

You can easily set the viewport scale by using the viewport scale pop-up located at the bottom right hand corner of the drawing editor. To set the scale of the drawing in the viewport relative to the size of the paper, select the viewport. Then, access the viewport scale pop up and select desired scale. If the desired scale is not present, you can also make a custom scale and add it to the existing list of scales.

Steps to making a custom scale:

1. Select the *scale drop down*.
2. Select *custom*.
3. Select *add*.
4. Enter the *scale name* and the *paper and drawing units*.
5. Select OK.

Setting the viewport scale changes the size of the drawing in the viewport based on the paper.

It is also important to take note of your scale format as it can be misundersood sometimes. A scale is often indicated in the format *plot size=actual size*. For example, ¼″=1′ this means that ¼ inch on the drawing, when plotted on paper represents 1 foot in actual life and on the drawing. If you are dealing with units, for example, 1:50, the same principles apply.

Plotting

The plot command allows you to plot a drawing. The plot command opens a dialog box that allows you to edit plot settings.

To access the plot menu, you can:

1. Type *plot* in the command line and hit enter
2. Select plot from the application menu

Layout/Paper Space

When plotting a drawing from paper space, there are some formalities that is needed to be observed. After setting up your paper space with title block, scale, viewport, page size, etc., it is time to plot. To commence the plotting sequence, you need to:

1. Right click on your paper space or layout tab and select *plot.*
2. Your plot dialog box will be displayed, double check your plot settings.
3. Select OK.

You can also plot multiple sheets at any single time from paper space. Follow these simple steps to achieve that result.

1. Right click on your paper space or layout tab and hit the option *select all layouts. (Note: All tabs will be highlighted)*
2. Right click and select *publish selected layouts.*

3. A publish dialog box is now open, you can organize and pick a location to save your file if it is PDF.

4. Once you have checked your document, select *publish.*

Note: *If you are plotting straight from your DWG file, ensure that your page size, orientation, plot style, and correct plotter is selected and then plot your drawing.*

<u>Model Space</u>

Plotting from model space is simple though it has not proven to be very accurate when it comes scaling your drawing. Once you set up your drawing with your title block and other amenities, go ahead to plot your drawing.

Follow these simple steps to plot from your model space.

1. Type plot in your command line and hit enter. The plot dialog box will appear.

2. Select your paper size, plotter, plot style, and orientation.

3. Under the plot area drop down, select *window. (This will take you back to the model space allowing you to highlight the area you wish to plot.)*

4. Select *preview* at the bottom left hand corner to see how the drawing appears on the sheet.

5. Once checks are completed, you can select OK and drawings will be plotted.

Ending the Program

You terminate the program by clicking on "A" then "Exit AutoCAD" in the lower right corner of the pull-down menu. The program will ask you if you want to save the changes you have made to the drawing. You should click the "Yes" button to save the changes.

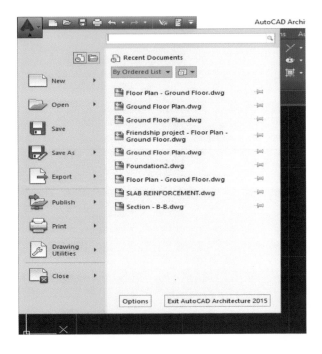

Acknowledgments

Credit to Ryan James for providing the idea to produce this book.

Editor: Aminata Coote

Sources

Jaiprakash Pandey. 150 AutoCAD Command and Shortcut list. https://thesourcecad.com/autocad-commands/

R. Greenlee. Introduction to AutoCAD. https://bit.ly/2kxvlP4

Ellen Finkelstein. 2011. AutoCAD 2012 and AutoCAD LT 2012 Bible. Indianapolis, IN. Wiley Publishing Inc.

George Omura. 2009. Mastering AutoCAD 2010 and AutoCAD LT 2010. Indianapolis, IN. Wiley Publishing Inc.

James Leach, Shawna Lockhart, Eric Tilleson. 2019. AutoCAD 2020 Instructor. Mission, KS. SDC Publications.

David Watson. Dimensioning. https://www.cadtutor.net/tutorials/autocad/dimensioning.php

Jaiprakash Pandey. Introduction to AutoCAD blocks and why you should use them. https://thesourcecad.com/free-cad-block/

Autodesk. 2018.AboutDesignCenter.https://autode.sk/2mfLHMH

Autodesk. 2018. Wblock. https://autode.sk/2khQDQz